Taxes on Home Businesses

Taxes on Home Businesses

Table Of Contents

Foreword

A lot of people today opt for starting their own home based business and popular as it is there should be some thought given to the tax breaks that one can and cannot enjoy through this form of business. Get all the info you need here.

Home Business Taxes

What You Need to Know About Taxes for a Home Based Business

Synopsis

The following are some areas worth looking into to gain more insight to the real facts of the tax breaks one can enjoy:

The Basics

Keeping a business journal that consist of all the details of the items that the individual has intentions of submitting for tax breaks would be done at the very onset of the business.

Being able to answer the tax auditors with proper documented proof can take a load off the stress and confusion that might otherwise occur. The more detailed the account the easier the process will be when addressing any queries.

Using the work space area as a tax deduction will also be something to consider and this should be calculated accurately and to the ratio of the premises being used for other purposes such as a dwelling place for the individual.

Any equipment that is being used for the purpose of conducting the business engine efficiently can also be factored into the tax deduction plan. These can be deducted in its original cost incurred state and depreciations are rarely expected to be taken into account.

Claims on savings for retirement plans, medical plans and social security deductions can also be given tax breaks.

The social security percentage can be calculated from the "employer" billing angle also one can include deductions made for any others assisting in the business.

Entertainment can also be a good area to consider for tax relief. Ensuring the entertainment is for business purposes and also to have the necessary backing proof would facilitate the smooth claiming procedure for such relief.

Any trips taken for business purposes can also be used to gain some percentage of tax relief. However there should be adequate documentation to substantiate the claim.

Chapter 2:

Getting Organized

Synopsis

Filling tax returns need not be a frustrating experience, if all the relevant documents are submitted along with the supporting claims for exceptions and reliefs. Preparing in advance by keeping good records will make the process easier and smoother thus easing the possible stress levels of the individual.

Get It Together

Perhaps the first thing to do is to file the tax forms early or on time and not leave it to the last minute where hundreds of things can go wrong due to the rush to get things done.

Having proper supporting documentations every step of the way is also another "do" point that should be taken seriously. Ensuring all ID numbers are filed with the application is also important as forgetting to include this can cause unnecessary delays and inconveniences.

Being self employed or having a home based business requires a little more work in terms of filling tax returns. All corresponding documentation should ideally be supported with the relevant receipts, bills, sales slips and any other business related expense notifications.

Areas that can be considered for claims would include office equipment, mileage records, business entertainment, supplies bought for the business, utilities and many other which a tax claims officer can indicate.

Using financial bank statements to make a comparison on the final deductions made and whether there are any discrepancies is another wide element to look into. Although most forms of savings have taxes linked to it, there are ways that can help to file relief for such accounts.

Mortgages are also another element that one can claim against when it comes to looking for tax relief. The payment made on the interest can be used to get added relief from tax payments.

If the business entity decides to support any charities or other similar kinds of needs such as volunteering for a good cause, this can also be a tax deduction platform for the individual.

Chapter 3:

Calculate Expenses

Synopsis

Reasonable deductions can be made for tax exceptions reasons and knowing how to go about making the right claims and filing them accordingly will help the individual keep the tax on the home business at a minimum.

The Output

Below are some areas where calculations can be done to ensure the optimization exercise of tax relief for the home based business entity:

- As in any other business the element is significant to the success of the business. It contributes to the awareness campaign of the product and getting the attention of the relevant masses for revenue earning purposes. Therefore most businesses would require some sort of business advertising budget which is tax deductable.

- Business start up cost is also another tax deductable possibility. Keeping a well documented account of these expenses incurred will enable the individual to file comprehensive and accurate tax required information.

- Legal, accounting and any other professional fees that may be incurred along the way because of the home business can also be calculated to be included in the tax relief claims.

- Communication tools can also be calculated into the claims exercise is this is a contributing factor that is part of the business engine.

- Utilities and rental can also be included however this may be a little complicated as the premise is also being used for other purposes such as a dwelling place.

- There is also a section that is termed as miscellaneous that can be used to calculate certain expenses incurred during the course of the business.

- Sometimes meals and entertainments are noted in this section but the receipts pertaining the occasion should be clearly indicative to the reason and who was present and why such an expense needed to be included.

- Though noted as a home based business there may be a requirement to travel and as such calculations can and should include this too.

Chapter 4:

Maximize Deductions

Synopsis

Being smart and savvy about how to manage and maximize deductions for tax exceptions is something that should be considered if the individual is interested in taking full advantage of the tax deduction possibilities.

The home business owner who is diligent about keeping track of every expense incurred during the course of the business will most likely be able to reap the benefits when it comes paying less taxes.

Maximize

The following tips are noted for the maximization of the deductions:

Keeping track of all business expenses and ensuring the relevant documentation is available to match these claims is very important.

Keeping a daily journal will prove to be very beneficial in the long run as it will more clearly show all activities thus providing a more solid case towards and claims of relief.

Crossing checking deductions against the different types of taxes will in some cases yield surprisingly positive results. Towards the end of the financial physical year, the individual should make a comparison of these different tax platforms which would include deciding between state income tax deductions or state sales tax deductions and choose the one most suited to gain the relevant relief.

Comparing itemized and overall deductions may not always be the best of decisions to make as in some cases opting for a more standard deduction filing may prove to be beneficial. Exploring the possibility of using different tax platforms for different deductions may also be a plausible thing to do.

Exploring beyond just the regular and customary possibilities is another option to look into when trying to maximize deductions.

Considering other unconventional areas that may allow tax exceptions such as medical and dental expenses, sales tax and personal property tax, educational expenses, damages caused by disaster which is crippling to the particular home business and many others.

Chapter 5:

Claim Your Health Insurance

Synopsis

Tax breaks for home businesses can also be gotten when filing on health insurance. This is not commonly practiced as most people are not aware that they can get deduction and relief for this sort of expenses. This is especially designed to help that smaller start up businesses and this often provides a lot of relief for those applying under this criteria.

Health Costs

Tax claims for relief can be done on health insurance and also on certain medical expenses incurred by the home business owner as an added help for the individual.

Filing for such claims can only be done if there are no other bodies paying out towards the medical claim submitted for the tax relief.

Claims also cannot be made if there is a possibility of the same claim being made in a compensatory form from other parties. This could in some cases be termed as fraud as payments for the same claim is being sought from different sources.

Other areas that the home based business owner may have difficulty is seeking tax relief would be for routine medical and dental care which are not life threatening in nature.

Claims can be made on prevention, diagnosis, alleviation or treatment of several different platforms or sections provided for within the medial perspective.

These include an ailment, an injury, an infirmity, a defect or a disability. It is not necessary to prove that these claims made were directly connective to the individual simply because he or she was operating a home based business.

Other areas where claims can be made would be such as doctors' and consultants' fees, diagnostic procedures which are often deemed to be carried out on the advice of the medical personnel taking the case, drug and medications prescribed by a doctor, dentist or medical consultant, and any physiotherapy or similar treatment that may be needed to right a medical problem.

Chapter 6:

Track Mileage

Synopsis

Mileage can also be another avenue where tax exemptions can be made to the benefit of the home business owner. As a good percentage of the business may require the individual to travel to meet clients or customers this form of relief can prove to be quite beneficial and rather substantial if claims are made and exploited to the maximum.

Mileage

The current tax system does make allowances for expenses charged for traveling and this comes in the form of mileage allowance payments.

Under this system the claims made on a per mile basis are not subject to income that is taxable if they are paid below the rate set by the governing body at the time.

Even if the vehicle used at the time is also for personal transportation use the tax relief calculated on the trips which were solely done for business reasons can be significant tax saving.

Adding to this there is also the overall further tax relief which can be gained through any mileage allowance payments made. The individual would have to calculate the total sum set aside in the tax year for such payments which will then be deducted from total earnings along with other expenses that attract the exemption possibility to create the total tax liability for the year.

Also to be noted is that the calculations are done on the total mileage allowance which has been set aside for the purpose of travelling for business purposes and not on the actual mileage used.

Therefore the tax relief enjoyed can be more even when the entire planned expense is not fully utilized.

For a more itemized directional help, it would be better to research available material on the subject to ensure that all possible angles are explored for the optimum saving possible from the tax on mileage incurred.

Chapter 7:

Synopsis

In the quest to explore various ways to exploit the tax relief systems in place the individual should spend some time exploring the area of retirement accounts. This retirement account possibility presents some interesting and applicable points that encourage the individual to save towards it because of the incentives given through the tax relief system.

Putting Money Aside

To reduce taxable income the home based business owner can make contributions towards a traditional individual retirement account otherwise referred to as IRA. These contributions can then be used to file for some tax relief. The contributions can be made as late as the first due date of a tax return. This can also be used as a retroactive contribution to the previous tax year.

There are two types of retirement fund possibilities to choose from which are the traditional IRA and the Roth IRA or in some cases both may be used, this all depends on the individual's aspirations during the retirement phase in life. As this foresight for the well being of the individual is also encouraged by any governing body the assistance given in the form of tax relief is meant to instill this important thought for the future.

Most people are eligible for such an allowance based on earned income and the IRA certainly encourages this as it also extends this facility to self employed individuals.

However there is an age limit which is anyone below the age of 70-5 years unlike the Roth IRA which does not have any such stipulations. In order to facilitate claims made there is no need to have extensive and itemized reports attached to the claims. Simply using the designated forms for the relevant purposes will suffice and facilitate the claims process. There are various levels of deductions which include full deductions, partial deductions and entire deductions and these are based on a variety of different factors.

Chapter 8:

Hire Family Members

Synopsis

Surprising but good to know is the fact that hiring the family to work in the home based business entity in not only a good idea but is also supported by the governing body of the time. This is clearly evident in the tax exemptions put in place to encourage and facilitate such undertakings.

Final Tips

Besides the obvious positive impacts it can have when the family is encouraged to work together as seen in the past, there is also the advantage of getting valuable tax relief.

Family members can be an excellent source to tap into if there is a certain amount of respect and compensation in place to acknowledge these contributions. They can be trustworthy, dedicated, inexpensive and other positive contributing characteristics to the business entity.

To top it all off there is the incentive of making tax relief claims for each of the expenses incurred through the employment of family members.

There is no need to pay federal unemployment taxes and there is also relief from withholding income taxes and paying payroll taxes and this also takes into account of not having to pay social security either until the age of 18 in the case of minors being employed.

The insurance taken out on the family members' contribution to the working of the business can also be cheaper and better with the added advantage of further tax reliefs in this area.

Wrapping Up

It is a known fact that it is sometimes hard to find tax exceptions outlets for smaller home based businesses as compared with large corporations who generally enjoy tax rebates in a big way. This is simply because the larger entities are more aware of their tax paying rights than the individual running the home based business. Therefore it is important to spend some time exploring the possibility of seeking this form of tax relief.